REVISED AND F

Busting the Retirement Lies

Understanding Prosperity Economics
to Thrive in Your Senior Years

prosperityeconomicsmovement

A Brief Guide by the Non-Profit Foundation
PROSPERITY ECONOMICS MOVEMENT

CONTENTS

With much gratitude to Andrew Chapman, Sue Hartnett, Dan Hays, Jim Kindred, Carmen Langford, Joe Marron, Andy McVeigh, Nancy McVeigh, Nelson Nash, Art Riedmann, Armin Sethna, Babs Smith, and Dan Sullivan.

INTRODUCTION

It's no surprise that the concept of retirement is nowhere to be found in ancient times or in ancient texts, including The Bible. In the Middle Ages, when people spoke of retiring, they meant either turning in for the night or retreating from the battlefront.

The word's usage in the current sense—"withdrawal from one's position or occupation or from active working life" (*Merriam-Webster Dictionary*, online)—is traced to the year 1590. But the term or concept came into popular usage less than 100 years ago, with the passing of the 1935 Social Security Act. And, according to two sources—the *Online Etymology Dictionary* and Dictionary.com—the word "retiree" is an "Americanism" that only came into use in the 1940s!

Busting the Retirement Lie is produced by The Prosperity Economics Movement in order to help people worldwide, but especially in the United States, re-think and—dare we say it?—*retire* our standard notions and expectations of retirement.

The Prosperity Economics Movement (PEM) is a nationwide effort to pull together financial advisors who practice the Seven

Principles of Prosperity™ and connect them with clients who want better results from their money. In our view, the almost universally applied model of quitting a job or career entirely at a certain age has never really worked for most people, cannot work, and—if we had our way—*should not* work for most people today.

Why do we say this? Three main reasons:

First, the very intent of retirement—when defined as "to take out of service" or "withdrawal from one's position or from active working life"—doesn't sound like fun at all.

Second, in our 20+ years in the financial services business, we've seen that most folks cannot financially afford to retire *and* maintain their accustomed standard of living.

Last but not least, from our experience with people who have retired and those who have not (you'll hear their stories along the way), we've learned that retirement just isn't good for you—physically, emotionally, psychologically, or mentally.

Let's examine each of our assertions above in a little more detail, shall we?

We believe human beings were put on earth to serve—first our families, then our communities, and more and more in this globally connected age, the world. When we stop serving and live a life that is focused on self, our lives can go downhill in a hurry, as shown in the movie *Ghost Town*, a 2008 New York Times Critics' Pick. Yes, the media has put forth the idea of one's "golden years" filled with golf and fishing, art and food, and plenty of travel. But we have it on good authority that the "fish don't clap" (see profile on O. Alfred Granum on page xiii).

Can we afford to retire? Obviously, some families build enough wealth during their working years to live off that resource base during their later years. But for most of us, the idea that we can save money from age 30 to 65 and then live off that money from age 65 to age 100—yes, age 100!—is financially unfeasible due to the effects of inflation and taxation. That doesn't include the reality that most Americans simply don't save enough from 30 to 65, nor do we save it very well. In other words, *where* we save our money tends to cause its loss, erode its growth, and limit its capability.

Retirement isn't good for your health. While there is still some debate about the effects of retirement on one's physical health, numerous studies have shown that an abrupt shift into retirement from working full-time can, and does, have negative impacts on mental and emotional health. Dan Hays (the author's father) can attest to that.

> Dan became a school teacher right when he got out of college and, eventually, worked many years as a school principal, until the age of 58. For a variety of reasons, including his wife's early passing, he retired. Living on the same 40-acre farm he had for many years, there were numerous tasks to keep him physically occupied. He was also very involved in his church. Yet, over time, he felt emotionally disconnected from the young people he was used to serving. He volunteered in a few classrooms and mentored a few student teachers. This helped, but there was still something missing. Then, when he was 69 years old, a local country charter school asked him to consult with them as they worked through some issues. That led to a part-time job as their principal and—while he's only supposed to put in 30 hours a week—he usually puts in 40+ hours because of the joy and energy he gets from serving again.

Likewise, most of us have seen stories after stories of athletes who "retire" and then make some very poor choices with their lives and their money. Some of them figure it out and start producing value again, generating both income and good will—but some of them don't and end up living unproductive lives or, worse, become a nuisance in society.

So, if we're suggesting that you shouldn't retire, what *should* you do instead? As the personal account of Art Riedmann at the end of this section illustrates, our book presents a number of steps, in six chapters summarized below, that might help you look forward to another productive and satisfying epoch in your life.

Match your purpose with your prowess. In other words, figure out what you're good at, as well as what your instinctive life or "soul" purpose is. There are several ways to do this, and we propose a few that we find particularly helpful.

Based on what you learn and know about yourself, **find work or volunteer opportunities you love.** Make lists of services you could provide and start doing so now. Some of them will earn money and some won't. But there are many entrepreneurial services that can be provided, and we'll share some ideas to get you thinking.

Strategize on how you can keep doing that work, both paid and unpaid, for the rest of your life.

Save 20% of your income. This advice goes back to biblical ages! Use it all along the way through your life for sabbaticals and long vacations and times when your work doesn't earn the money you'd like to have.

Think about living beyond 100 years. Science is beginning to learn that our lifespans are largely self-limited due to our ways of living. As medicine and technology discover more about how we can improve our lifestyles for longevity, we can make better choices. More people are living past the 100-year mark now than ever before—and more will be doing so with each passing year.

Get excited, stay excited, and help others do the same. Human beings were built to push our limits a bit, so consider pushing yourself at least once each week to stay engaged in life. Plus, take special note of those things that energize you and bring you enthusiasm, whether big or small, and incorporate them into your life more. Lastly, encourage the people around you to do the same.

Retirement Profile: Arthur C. Riedmann (1921–)
A Personal Account

There are usually a number of factors involved when someone decides to keep working after reaching the age of 65. Those particular to me were:

1. My dear wife (of 57 years) and I had decided before marriage that we would like to have a large family. We were blessed with an answer to our prayers, and our family now includes four sons and five daughters. When I reached age 65, our home was still active with the presence of three of our children, as they continued with their high school and university educations.

2. My parents were German immigrants, with the work ethic of that nation, and it was passed on to me—my father didn't retire until age 72. I also liked my job, which consisted of affording commercial property and liability coverages to major clients. The work was interesting and challenging, and with my professional degree in that industry, it was a good fit. This work ethic was also passed on to my only sibling—my brother, who became a Franciscan priest and continued some of his priestly duties until age 90. Now 96, he is in a clerical home for the aged in New Jersey.

3. My third consideration was financial. The insurance business is steady and afforded us the opportunity to always have a nice, clean, and happy home. At the same time, raising a family of nine did not permit much attention to retirement plans, nor were they typical in the industry in those days. So my period from age 65 to retirement at age 76 gave me an opportunity to finally pay more attention to that subject.

Plans for after retirement

Prior to retirement, I had joined the St. Vincent de Paul Society and delivered food boxes to the needy on Saturdays. After retirement, I intended to stay active, and volunteering was my solution. My wife and I were able to work weekdays delivering food boxes. Osborn School District began the Oasis program, which consisted of people my age helping children to improve their reading skills, and I was an original member of the program. I also joined Ozanam Manor, a transitional housing shelter for the homeless, as an interviewer and subsequently a mentor. We assisted our clients for up to six months, ultimately helping them return to society. Another enjoyable volunteering activity was ushering in Symphony Hall in downtown Phoenix. But sorry to say, age does take its toll, so my sole volunteering activity now is the weekly watering of the front of our building (one of six) that composes our condominium community.

Staying physically active

My entire childhood in Brooklyn seemed to consist of sports activities. There were always enough children available on our street to start a game, and we played whatever was appropriate to the season: mostly hockey on roller skates, but also basketball and softball. There has never been a time in my life to vegetate—even now, my wife and I swim each day in our condominium pool, usually from April until the end of September. During the other six months of the year, we take daily walks. And tending to our rose garden and incidental activities satisfactorily fills the rest of the days.

I believe the above would indicate a successful life to the reader. But it would be missing the fact that a spiritual outlook was the glue that held all this together. My wife and I attend Mass almost daily and thank God always for his blessings. The result is happiness—which we wish for all, especially for our family and anyone reading this attempt at retirement wisdom.

Retirement Profile: O. Alfred Granum (1922–)
Legend Still Enjoys Seven-Decade Career

Al Granum, the leading light of Northwestern Mutual Life who developed the revolutionary One Card System of financial planning advisory services, was an active teacher, author, and speaker until he retired. His love of fishing, however, wasn't enough to keep him hooked on retirement—he missed the interaction, the connection, and yes, the "applause," when he helped others through his speaking engagements. So, back he went to work and, at the age of 90, still goes into the offices at his company, Granum Agency Inc., nearly every day.

Source: http://www.lifehealthpro.com/2009/05/06/the-keen-insight-of-al-granum

CHAPTER 1

MATCH YOUR PURPOSE WITH YOUR STRENGTHS

"At an early age, you started hearing it: It's a virtue to be 'well-rounded.' ... They might as well have said: Become as dull as you possibly can be."

—*Donald O. Clifton in his book* Living Your Strengths: Discover Your God-Given Talents and Inspire Your Community

Each of us has an "instinctive purpose" that makes us happy. In the rushed world of work and family, perhaps just a few of us know what that purpose is. Some of us may have forgotten what it is; some of us haven't discovered it yet.

But it is this purpose, when combined with the skills we've developed and nurtured over time, or even those skills we may have put aside and think we've forgotten, that gives us the basis to live productive, meaningful, satisfying lives.

We cannot recommend highly enough the Kolbe System™—see www.Kolbe.com—as a means to helping you find how you can achieve a successful balance between what you'd like to do and what you are able to do. The founder of the Prosperity Economics Movement was introduced to Kathy Kolbe's insightful life's work in the mid-1990s via The Strategic Coach Program. Even though the Kolbe Corp's office was right down the street (and an internationally known company), she was unaware of the dramatic impact that Kolbe was having on lives, helping people realize that they have the ability to express their innate or God-given talents. Originally focusing on techniques to help students navigate the educational process and develop their skills, Kolbe's approach expanded to adults—in organizations and as individuals.

As Kolbe says, "Success is the freedom to be yourself." Yet, knowing yourself is one of the hardest things to do. We strongly encourage you to go to Kolbe.com and spend the $50 and 20 minutes to take the Kolbe A™ Index. (For those under age 18, there is the Kolbe Y™ for only $10.) This insightful tool will give you specifics on how *you* work to get results and help you know whether you are seeking out the right opportunity, be it paid employment or as a volunteer. With this knowledge in hand, your search and finding a match will be easier. When you are doing work you love, it no longer feels like work.

Another tool we've found helpful is available at www.Strengths-Finder.com. Developed over a period of several decades by Donald O. Clifton, "the father of strengths-based psychology," the Strengths-Finder assessment is based on 34 "themes" or strengths. This diagnostic tool helps individuals identify five main strengths, on the premise that building on strengths is much easier than trying to improve weaknesses.

For Kim Butler, founder of the Prosperity Economics Movement, knowing these (in addition to the information she obtained from the Kolbe assessment) helped identify the specific areas of her profession that most closely connect her strengths with how she gets results. For example, one of her strengths is achievement. Knowing this helped her realize why, even on a Saturday, she needs to feel like she's *accomplished something*. Yet, because she is a devotee of The Strategic Coach's "free day" concept (see Chapter 5), she wants her Saturdays to be free from business. So, through trial and

The trademarks listed are the trademarks of Kolbe Corp.

error, she found a few things she can do that aren't business related, yet give her a sense accomplishment. In the summer, for example, she spends many hours mowing pastures and doing farm work, while in the winter she crochets the alpaca fiber that her animals produce.

Retirement Profile: Jeanne Robertson (1945–) Loving Life—and Laughing at It, Too!

Jeanne Robertson has been making a living looking at the lighter side of life for nearly 50 years. And now in her late 60s, she shows no signs of stopping her career of motivational speaking at conventions and corporate gatherings around the country. In fact, in the last three years, she has added a whole new digital dimension to her work, following a clip of one of her stories that was posted on YouTube and went viral.

The six-foot-two 1963 Miss North Carolina figured out she had a knack for public speaking—with a humorous twist—while delivering over 500 speeches in the year after winning the title. (She also went on to win Miss Congeniality in the Miss America pageant later that year.)

According to one reporter, "While other people her age may be thinking about retirement, for Robertson that is not an option right now. She said the Internet has opened up a world of opportunities she never expected, so as long as she can deliver and as 'long as the lights are down low to look pretty good out there,' she said, she will be on stage. 'It's a whole new world and I am embracing it,' she added." ("Living on the edge," by Keren Revas, *The Burlington Times-News*, Sept. 6, 2009.)

In addition to her live speeches and performance, Robertson makes extensive use of online media through marketing short, downloadable clips on iTunes. She's learned how to title her stories so they appeal to Internet viewers and has linked up with Sirius XM radio, which plays her stories several times each day on the family comedy channel.

Robertson's secret to keeping her material fresh is keeping a journal. According to the *Time-News* article, "'Everything that happens in my life that is funny goes into the journal,' she said. 'Though not everything that happens in life is funny, if you look hard, you will find that a lot of it is…. In the 1960s, I was talking about beauty pageants…. Now, I am talking about getting older.'"

Retirement Profile: W. Edwards Deming (1900–1993) A Passion for Quality—a Life-Lesson from a Business Philosopher

The founding "guru" of systems thinking and quality management, this unassuming man from Laramie, Wyoming, turned around the fortunes of the likes of the Ford Motor Company and post-war Japanese industries. And he was still doing this, through management seminars and workshops, until just 10 days before his passing in December 1993.

Dr. Deming's experiences in Japan, focusing on improving product durability and reliability, had a lasting impact on that country's emergence from the post-war destruction and poverty. In fact, his name and fame in Japan were second only to that of Gen. Douglas MacArthur. Yet Deming remained little known or respected in the United States well into the 1970s—as American industry equated better quality with higher cost.

Only when Japanese electronics and automobiles started making inroads into the American market in the 1970s and 1980s, did the U.S. industry sit up and take notice. The Ford Motor Company was one of the first to seek Mr. Deming's help. Executives were not pleased when he told them that 85% of quality problems are the result of management errors. But, under his patient tutelage, Ford focused on quality improvement with eventual and obvious success. Other companies then turned to Deming, including Xerox, Dow Chemical, AT&T, and *The New York Times*.

Is it surprising then that, with such a passion for quality, Deming himself lived a life of quality? "Well into his 90s," according to *The New York Times*, "Mr. Deming maintained an active travel schedule, crisscrossing the country to conduct seminars and consult with companies he considered sufficiently motivated to benefit from his attention. He also lectured at Columbia University's Business School and taught continuously at New York University's Stern School of Business from 1946 until the end of the spring term this year." (Joshua Holusha, Dec. 21, 1993, *The New York Times*)

What if we paid a little more attention to the *quality* of what we do and how we think?

CHAPTER 2

FIND WORK YOU LOVE

"Retirement is the ugliest word in the language."

—Ernest Hemingway

Have you ever had a day when you just lazed around the house all day, thinking that would rejuvenate you?

Did it?

For some, yes; but for most, probably no.

As human beings, we were put on this earth to serve and add value. But one challenge is knowing ourselves well enough to find work that is so connected to our individual strengths and our "instinctive" way of achieving results that we can't wait to get up every morning.

Simply put, we need to find work we *love*—whether it's full-time, part-time, flex-time, freelance, phased, sabbatical, seasonal, paid, personal, volunteer, or whatever.

For help in this area, explore www.InstinctiveLife.com, run by Tammi Brannan. Brannan's strength is helping others figure out their purpose in life—a broader concept that can help people of any age define how they can best spend their days. When we are aware of our purpose and conscious of our strengths, it is much easier to find work (whether paid or volunteer) that matches who we are, so we can stay excited about it. The process of discovering (or in some cases, re-discovering) your "instinctive life" can be quite a spiritual journey, and Brannan offers tools to guide you along the way.

Learning can be exciting, and humans *want* to learn. We are programmed for it. And we are best situated for learning when the topic fits in with our life purpose in some way. This leads to natural curiosity. When we are curious about the subject matter, it's much easier to be excited about work, as well as the learning required to do well at that work. As you can see, this goes full circle—your life purpose leads to topic interest, which leads to curiosity, which leads to excitement, which leads to learning, which is fulfilling to our life purpose. This makes us happier people while working, and happier at home and during off hours. Thus, if you view work as something you'll do your entire life, rather than as drudgery to be endured for a few decades, you'll take the time to find the right fit. Thankfully, in today's economy, changing jobs is normal. So, keep changing until you find what's right for you.

Additionally, make a list of services you could provide, based on your talents and, most importantly, what you love—and start providing them now. What you have to offer is needed, even if you don't think so. These may be services you perform simply because you love doing them or because they bring in a little extra money, but you may find they lead to a full-time business or other opportunity. And because you are operating within a "space" that you love, whatever opportunities and connections come your way are more likely to fit well with your instinctive purpose.

That is why we suggest a list of services you would *enjoy* doing. Each of us has things we like to do. When you put them all together you get a literal world of possibilities. Thankfully, everything that needs to be done matches up with people who like to do it. (Yes, there really are people that like mowing the lawn and doing paper-work.) And it doesn't have to be income related—find others in your community who like to do the things you don't like to do, and vice versa, and trade with them. You can even start a barter circle, which is a list of members and each one's talents, through which each member can exchange services. It can even extend between more than two people, such as when Person A performs a service for Person B, who does something for Person C, who then does something for Person A.

A shining example of creatively matching individuals' time and services with needs in their immediate communities is Seniors Helping Seniors. This for-profit model matches demand with supply and helps keep experienced, older adults active and earning money—assisting peers with whom they can relate in a variety of tasks related to daily living or just for basic human companionship. We encourage you to explore www.SeniorsHelpingSeniors.com, which will give you a better idea of what can be done for others—and, in the bargain, for yourself.

CHAPTER 3

STRATEGIZE ON HOW YOU CAN WORK FOR THE REST OF YOUR LIFE

**"Retirement at sixty-five is ridiculous.
When I was sixty-five I still had pimples."**

—George Burns

Retirement usually takes place at age 65. Where did that number come from?

"Your 65th birthday is nothing more than an arbitrary line scratched across your life by someone else for reasons that have nothing to do with you or your well-being." That's the blunt and pretty accurate view of blogger MelP, who goes on to note: "Historically, retirement has been nothing more than a tool for getting older people out of the way. It is bad for older people, middle-aged workers, and society as a whole. It is time to re-think the whole notion." (MelP, Oct. 13, 2009, "Time to Retire the Concept of Retirement," http://www.thenexthill.com/time-to-retire-the-concept-of-retirement.html)

We feel strongly that laws in the United States need to be changed so that forced retirement does not continue to occur. For example, we have clients who were forced to retire at a certain age by "company rules"—rules written long ago, when a certain age was believed to come with limitations. Thankfully, now when people keep their health up with daily activity and good eating habits, most of us have no physical or mental reason to stop working. It is sad to see people who love their work, and are skilled and experienced at it, asked to leave just because of their age.

Experience counts in a variety of ways and it can be very beneficial for companies to retain experienced people. If you fit this category, consider talking with your employer about working fewer hours, job-sharing, working from home, or the other options available that give variety to the typical 40-hour workweek. That way, you can enjoy life a bit more—think three-day weekends every week—*and* keep working. Just be sure to pitch your ideas to your employer with some benefit for the company; if it is only about what's to your advantage, it is less likely to be well received. If you aren't sure how your proposed arrangement could be good for the company, talk with trusted coworkers who might be in a position to offer suggestions—while keeping your plans quiet.

Alternatively, consider quitting your job and taking extended time off with the idea of coming back and consulting for the company on your time schedule. Carmen Langford, who is in her early 70s, did that as head of microbiology for the local hospital in Nacogdoches, Texas. Now she works about three days a week—sometimes less, sometimes more—and focuses only on the things she enjoyed the most in her former work. In addition, because she is a paid consultant, she can take longer vacations or not go to work on any given day if she doesn't want to.

The movie industry has long operated in this manner. Skilled contributors, from directors to the actors to stunt women to extras, editors, and camera crew come together to work on a particular movie, then go their separate ways. In between they may not work at all or they may find other similar work. During production they may be busier than they would like, but they know it won't last forever so they handle it.

However, one thing to remember is the need to keep flexible, be willing to adjust your skill set, and not fear the future. Dennis Stearns, head of the Stearns Financial Services Group in North Carolina, spoke recently about eight trends that have the potential to add a trillion dollars to the global economy. Reporting on Mr. Stearns's presentation at a regional meeting of the Association of Financial Planners meeting in San Francisco in 2012, financial writer Bob Veres highlighted a couple of the major themes from the presentation:

> … an exploding market for retraining and skill development, due to the U.S. structural unemployment (people untrained for the jobs that are in high demand) as the workforce shifts from farm to factory to a technology / healthcare-based economy.
>
> "The bad news," said Stearns, "is that an estimated 30% or more of all of today's careers will be marginalized or cease to exist in the next eight to ten years. The good news is that we will also have 30% or more that will be invented, that don't exist today."
>
> The losers in this trend will be people who are not good at adapting or retooling their skill sets, and any college kids who party through their first couple of years of college....
>
> Stearns offered a seventh theme that might be called soft innovation.... Stearns [told] the audience to expect new consumer-friendly improvements in cars, the Internet, household appliances, etc.
>
> The winners will be any innovative company that uses the technological innovations creatively to shift buying habits dramatically in their favor.
>
> (*Inside Information*, July 2012)

To remain relevant, to truly keep and feel "alive," transformation and change are essential. To sum up, we quote author and businessman Bruce Barton (1886-1967):

"When you're through changing, you're through."

"I work part time and don't make a lot of money, but I save a ton because I don't have time to shop anymore!"
—*Sue Hartnett, retired and then went back to work*

Retirement Profile: Andrew A. McVeigh (1921–2011)
A Discovery of Regret

My father, Andrew A. McVeigh, retired at the age of 65. He had been employed by Armour Foods for 35 years and Swift Foods for 7 years. At the time of his retirement, he had been a plant manager of a pork slaughterhouse in South Dakota for approximately 11 years. He took an aged plant that had been budgeted to lose substantial amounts of money and turned it into one of the most successful plants in the company. We always thought that my father enjoyed his retirement—two and a half decades when he passed away. But in a conversation with him towards the end of his life, I was surprised to learn otherwise. While we were talking one day, he told me that retiring early was one of the worst decisions he had ever made and he regretted it. If he could have done it over, he would have continued to work for five to ten more years. He said that during his first years of retirement he was depressed and bored, not sure what to do with his time. Eventually, he became very involved at church, with a local food bank, and some other activities and worked his way out of his funk.

The lesson for others is to reconsider your vision of retirement. Think long and hard about what it will mean for you, given your personality. If you are highly active and involved in your work, don't suddenly bring it to a complete halt. You can't do something for most of your life, have it abruptly end, and expect no loss of purpose. If your career or work must come to an end as you know it, plan on replacing it with lesser work or volunteer activities—leisure alone doesn't typically provide long-term satisfaction. Even if you have not been highly active in your career or have been dreaming of days void of any obligations, a sudden lack of purpose or direction may be more challenging than you think.

—Andy McVeigh

CHAPTER 4

SAVE 20% OF YOUR INCOME

"The question isn't at what age I want to retire, it's at what income."

—*George Foreman*

We suggest 20% rather than the usual 10–15% because we want you to use your saved money along the way, and not just leave it to the ravages of inflation. The present value calculator below shows us how inflation has such a devastating effect on saved money. Let's say you work for one of those companies that still has a defined benefit pension, and you are close to age 65. You're thinking of retiring because you've been told your pension will be $3,000 a month and you know you can live on that.

Well, the bad news is, $3,000 a month today will feel like $924 a month in 30 years.

You'll notice we chose a 4% inflation rate. Let's try 9% and see what that does.

Future Value:	3,000		Title	Clear	N
Annual Payment:	0		· Beg	End	E W
Annual IRate:	9.00%		A M Q S		T
Years:	30.00				O P
Present Value:	226.11				

OUCH!

Even though the check will still read $3,000, it will only spend like $226 if inflation averages 9%. The only way to solve this problem is to have more money or earn more income. Inflation is like a stealth tax because we don't really see it on a statement anywhere. Furthermore, the U.S. government identifies a "basket of goods and services" every so often that it uses to define inflation by measuring how much change there has been in the costs of those goods and services. But the problem is, the contents of this "basket" keep changing which, in turn, affects the data.

Given the impact of inflation, the typical thinking of "work for 30 years, then retire for 30 or more years" is faulty. Let's look at a Future Requirements Calculator from Truth Concepts on the next page. Truth Concepts provides calculators nationwide to the Prosperity Economics Advisors who want to tell the whole truth to their clients about how money works and what is *really* going on with various types of products and strategies. The calculators are available for purchase by anyone, and if you like this kind of information, you might enjoy the blog on that site (www.TruthConcepts.

com). If you'd like the help of an advisor who works in this area, go to www.MountainTopsEducation.com, fill in your information, and one of their advisors will respond quickly.

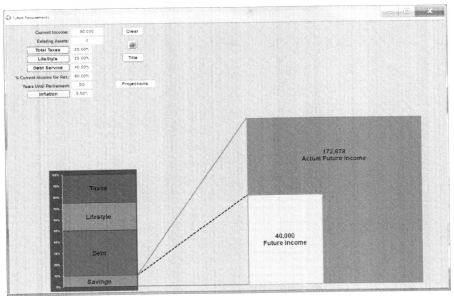

What this is telling us is that if we are:
- earning $50,000 a year,
- have no existing assets,
- only saving 10% a year,
- age 30,
- going to work to age 60, and
- inflation is 5%,

then we would have to have an annual income of $172,878 (and rising at 5%) to maintain our life style at the 80% level most financial planners assume. This 80% of current income for retirement is a major problem since most people don't want to reduce their life style to retire, yet we see "financial plans" that use 70% to 80% all the time.

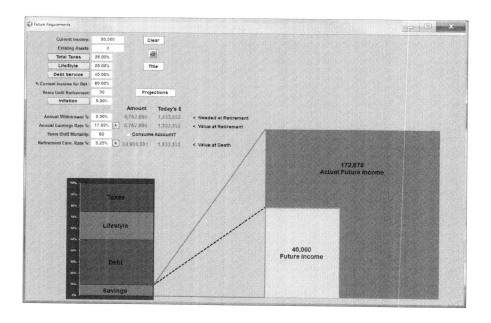

Yet it gets worse when we add the "Retirement" part to the equation. Looking at the graphic above, you can see we've set the Annual Withdrawal at 3%. That means we'd need to have $5,762,590 in an account (worth only $1,333,333 today) to generate that 80% of $172,878 annual income. In order to do this, we'd need to earn *17.53% on that account every single year without any fluctuation.*

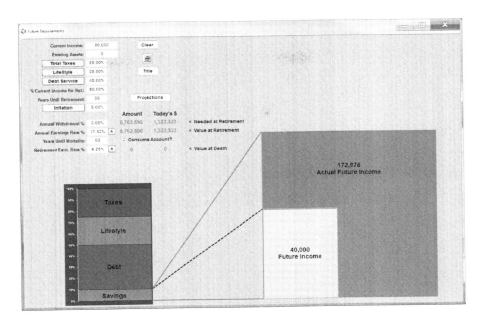

Furthermore, in order to live that same life style (with income rising annually by 5% to meet inflation) from age 60 to 90, that account would have to grow to $24,905,581 by age 90, during which time it would need to earn 8.25% annually. If we consumed the account and didn't leave anything for inheritance, it would only have to grow at 4.25%, as shown above.

The previous examples were just a fraction of the many major lies the financial planning industry puts forth. Others include:

Faulty assumptions

Financial planning makes assumptions about your future in ways that may be mathematically correct but are not realistic. Assuming interest rates, tax rates, inflation rates, and time frames can be very dangerous in that it can provide a false peace of mind. The graphs and charts may be pretty, but they don't reflect life. Since our society today changes so fast, it is ridiculous to assume anything will stay the same for more than a few years.

Misleading averages

Financial planning uses averages, which can be extremely misleading. We'll share an exaggerated example below to prove this point. This cash-flow calculator is, again, from www.TruthConcepts.com. Pretend someone offers you a mutual fund with an average return of 25%. Sounds pretty good (until you see how averages are calculated and what they do to money). So, you put $100,000 in the fund and watch for two years to get your results.

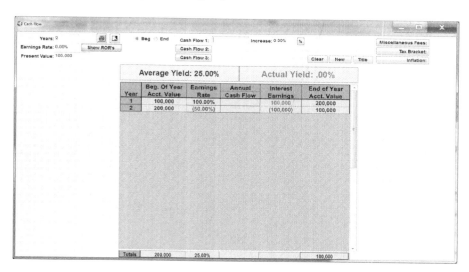

You can see the average yield is in fact 25%, but your *actual* yield is 0% because you still only have your $100,000. This is because your fund earned 100% in the first year and *negative 50%* in the second year. Quick math shows that 100% plus negative 50% divided by 2 equals 25%.

To put it another way, $100,000 earning 100% for year one grows to $200,000, but then gets cut in half when the fund loses 50% in the second year. So at the end of the second year, you are back to the $100,000 you started with—although the "statistics" show that your "average yield" was 25%. This is how the mutual fund industry calculates their returns!

Okay, you might say, at least you haven't lost any money. But let's now include fees and taxes and inflation (in the chart below) so you can see the *whole truth*.

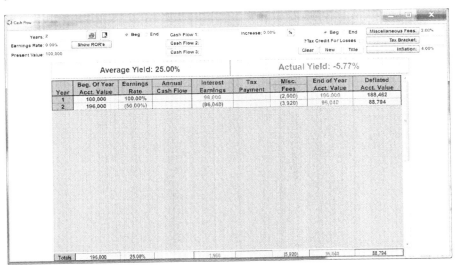

On the top right, we've set fees at 2%, taxes at 25% (a blended rate of income and capital gains for this example), and inflation at 4%. Notice your account is now only worth $77,922 and *you've actually lost 11.73%*. Hardly the 25% average you'd hoped for or expected.

Guessing about your age of retirement and passing

Financial planning assumes you know when you will want to stop working and also that you know when you will die. Both are really total guesses and yet they are used to make major decisions around life and money. The government dictates we *can't touch* our retirement dollars until age 59½ and then we *have to* start using them at 70½. But what do these ages have to do with our lives in any way? They are simply arbitrary and arguably outdated.

Statistics are showing more and more adults in the United States living past age 100. Yet, most financial plans still assume death at 85 or 90. We can look at a male age 60 on a life expectancy chart, yet that only means a *50% chance* that he will die by the life expectancy year listed (age 82, as shown in the chart below). Likewise, the longer you live, the longer you are likely to live—while the 60-year-old man in the chart below has a 50% chance of living to age 82, the 75-year-old man in the chart has a 50% chance of living to nearly age 88.

© 2001 Commissioners Standard Ordinary Mortality Table

☑ Male ☑ Standard ☑ Composite Joint Life Expectancy Table
○ Female ○ Preferred ○ NonSmoker Mortality 1   Mortality 2
Age: __ ○ SuperPreferred ○ Smoker

Age	L.E.	Age	L.E.	Age	L.E.	Age	L.E.
60	22.13	90	4.42	120	0.50		
61	21.44	91	3.90				
62	20.78	92	3.49				
63	20.12	93	3.15				
64	19.45	94	2.96				
65	18.79	95	2.78				
66	18.15	96	2.62				
67	17.51	97	2.47				
68	16.86	98	2.32				
69	16.28	99	2.19				
70	15.61	100	2.19				
71	15.01	101	2.19				
72	14.57	102	2.19				
73	14.12	103	2.19				
74	13.62	104	2.19				
75	12.92	105	2.19				
76	12.27	106	2.19				
77	11.99	107	2.19				
78	11.03	108	2.19				
79	10.51	109	2.19				
80	9.92	110	2.19				
81	9.34	111	2.19				
82	8.80	112	2.18				
83	8.21	113	2.16				
84	7.64	114	2.14				
85	7.09	115	2.08				
86	6.56	116	1.99				
87	6.01	117	1.84				
88	5.48	118	1.58				
89	4.95	119	1.16				

Source: American Academy of Actuaries

You'll notice the previous table is from the *2001* Mortality Table used by the life insurance industry. They don't update their tables very often, so it's easy to see how this information could already be outdated at the writing of this book in 2012. Bottom line: You'll probably live longer than you think. In order to have a higher quality of life for a longer time, you'll want to work as long as possible so you have the extra money to combat inflation and to keep yourself energized.

Not realistically accounting for inflation

Speaking of combating inflation, the longer money sits, the more impact inflation has on it. See this happening in the chart below, representing an existing $100,000 account where $20,000 a year is being added and a 4% inflation rate applied.

Look near the bottom of the table, at year 25, and you can see that while your account statement would read $600,000, it would feel as if you only had $225,070.

Year	Beg. Of Year Acct. Value	Earnings Rate	Annual Cash Flow	Interest Earnings	End of Year Acct. Value	Deflated Acct. Value
1	100,000		20,000		120,000	115,385
2	120,000		20,000		140,000	129,438
3	140,000		20,000		160,000	142,239
4	160,000		20,000		180,000	153,865
5	180,000		20,000		200,000	164,385
6	200,000		20,000		220,000	173,869
7	220,000		20,000		240,000	182,380
8	240,000		20,000		260,000	189,979
9	260,000		20,000		280,000	196,724
10	280,000		20,000		300,000	202,669
11	300,000		20,000		320,000	207,866
12	320,000		20,000		340,000	212,363
13	340,000		20,000		360,000	216,207
14	360,000		20,000		380,000	219,441
15	380,000		20,000		400,000	222,106
16	400,000		20,000		420,000	224,241
17	420,000		20,000		440,000	225,884
18	440,000		20,000		460,000	227,069
19	460,000		20,000		480,000	227,828
20	480,000		20,000		500,000	228,193
21	500,000		20,000		520,000	228,193
22	520,000		20,000		540,000	227,856
23	540,000		20,000		560,000	227,207
24	560,000		20,000		580,000	226,270
25	580,000		20,000		600,000	225,070
Totals	580,000		500,000			

Trying to beat inflation with savings

Another financial planning lie says if you increase your savings rate by the inflation rate every year, you'll beat the inflation problem. However, as you can see above, inflation works on the *whole account value*, so simply inflating your savings rate doesn't solve the problem. The only things that solve the problem are more money at work or more *you* at work for a longer time.

Here, even though you were increasing your $20,000 annual additions by 4% every year, you still weren't able to make the account feel like the present-value $881,652 it was supposed to feel like. (Actually, it should feel like more, because the $20,000-per-year savings were increased every year.) Instead, it feels like $349,953.

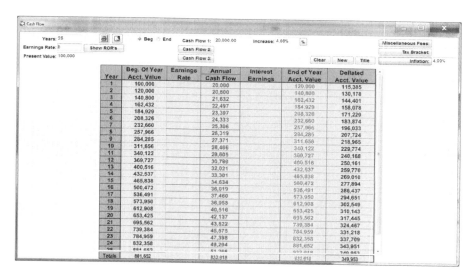

Again, the only solution? More money at work, or more *you* at work for a longer time.

If you want to read about more these lies and what to do about them in your financial world, find our book *Busting the Financial Planning Lies* at www.Partners4Prosperity.com/bfpl.

CHAPTER 5

THE REALITY OF
RETIREMENT PLANS

"Age is only a number, a cipher for the records. A man can't retire his experience. He must use it."

—Bernard Baruch, American financier, investor, philanthropist, and statesment

Now we'll switch to busting the lies of 401(k) plans (and their cousins, the 403(b), IRA, etc). First, we'll look conceptually at the idea with an "opportunity filter" we use to measure or "test" all investments. These 7 Principles of Prosperity are well known within the Prosperity Economics Movement and used by both advisors and clients nationwide to consider various opportunities. The goal is to determine whether or not a particular opportunity or investment warrants further examination from a numerical standpoint. We believe these ancient principles are time tested and have existed in economics since biblical times. You can read similar principles in *The Richest Man in Babylon* by George S. Clason.

The 7 Principles of Prosperity are as follows:

1. **Think**—Owing a prosperity mindset eliminates poverty; scarcity thinking keeps you stuck.
2. **See**—Increase your prosperity by adopting a macro-economic point of view: a perspective in which you can see how one of your economic decisions affects all the others. Avoid micro-economic "tunnel-vision."

3. **Measure**—Awareness and measurement of opportunity costs enables you to recover them. Ignore this at your peril.
4. **Flow**—The true measure of prosperity is cashflow. Don't focus on net worth alone.
5. **Control**—Those with the gold make the rules; stay in control of your money rather than relinquishing control to others.
6. **Move**—The velocity of money is the movement of dollars through assets. Movement accelerates prosperity; accumulation slows it down. Avoid accumulation.
7. **Multiply**—Prosperity comes readily when your money "multiplies," meaning that one dollar does many jobs. Your money is disabled when each dollar performs only one or two jobs.

One fallacy of the 401(k) plan is that somehow there will be more money to spend since we got the "tax deduction."

When we closely evaluate commonly held beliefs, sometimes they hold up… and sometimes they don't. Let's use the 7 Principles of Prosperity as a way to evaluate the all-American proposition for maximizing retirement savings: the 401(k).

In 1978, Congress amended the Internal Revenue Code by adding section 401(k), with the law going into effect in 1980. It was designed to allow a worker to save for retirement and have the savings invested, while deferring income taxes on the money saved (and on the earnings) until withdrawal. Sounds great, and many American workers agreed: by the mid-2000s well over a half a million businesses offered 401(k)s to their employees.

The employer sets up the Qualified Retirement Plans, so although there are similarities, there can be some real differences between yours and a friend's at another company. Choices abound, such as what the investment options are, in-service access (whether you can borrow from it or not), and employer match, just to name a few.

Over the past thirty years, the perceived value of the 401(k) to the average American worker has become so entrenched in the psyche of business leaders that a company's 401(k) is now considered a minimum requirement for recruiting and retaining employees.

But let's challenge the assumption that they are, in fact, a prosperity builder. We'll use The 7 Principles of Prosperity Test to evaluate the 401(k).

1. **Let's ask ourselves, does this investment vehicle eliminate or reduce poverty thinking and lifestyle?**

   A: Yes

   B: No

   Well, the answer is no… living an impoverished existence to save for the future on the premise that the joys of retirement will outweigh all the lost opportunities for enjoyment, investment, and growth is a poverty perspective.

2. **Let's consider that macro-perspective (at the 40,000-foot view). How does this decision affect your personal economic situation?**

   A: It improves it

   B: It doesn't

   Well, it *sounds* like it might improve it. You put some money away for retirement, and when you are ready to leave the working world, it's there for you. But hold on a second. Things start looking quite different when you consider that (a) your income will be fully taxable at an unknown to-be-determined rate; (b) you could lose your social security benefits; (c) it won't provide any disability protection if you are hurt and can no longer stay employed; (d) you can't collateralize it; and (e) your information is made public in the ERISA Red Book. (More about this "book" later.)

3. **Are you aware of the opportunity costs of putting your money into a 401(k)? Have you measured them?**
   A: Yes
   B: No
   The answer is *maybe*. You might be aware of your opportunity costs, but if you really *are* measuring them, then you'd see this one as a no-brainer. By putting the money from your earnings into the 401(k), you are giving up the capital-gain tax treatment and the money is not liquid, so you can't redeploy it for any other investment or use. The costs of your investments and the lack of liquidity are both major problems.

4. **Does the opportunity result in cash stagnating or flowing?**
   A: Flowing
   B: Stagnating
   This one is clear. The 401(k) plan promotes a *hoarding mentality*. You are looking to benefit from compounding interest, so the "law of cashflow" is being violated. Remember: locking that capital up is helpful *for your financial advisors* but detrimental to you and your financial security, power, and prosperity potential.

5. **Will you remain in control of your capital with a 401(k) or lose control of it?**
   A: Remain in Control
   B: Lose Control
   Again, simple: You'll lose control of it. You won't have the opportunity to leverage it for collateral for other investments unless you want to "borrow" it (basically from yourself) at a steep cost and possible penalty. And if you do decide to

borrow from your 401(k), you are limited in the amount and you will be given specific repayment terms with a structured loan. So, when you consider that you want "one dollar doing lots of jobs," this one is in sheer violation of this principle. Not only that, you also lose control over specifically WHERE you invest it and WHEN you distribute it.

6. **Does this opportunity enable the velocity of money through your assets or toward them?**

   A: It moves

   B: It accumulates

   This test is pretty self-evident, too. Money accumulates here and is not moving at all. When it isn't moving, it cannot go "through" assets, it can only go "toward" them.

7. **Does your money do several "jobs" with this opportunity or only one?**

   A: Several jobs

   B: Only one

   Only one or two jobs here, and the tax-deferral benefit, as we already discussed, is really not a job at all—it's just a way to delay the inevitable.

So, please consider your retirement planning carefully. With 401(k)s, IRAs, SEP plans, Keogh plans, pensions, profit-sharing, and Defined Benefit Plans, you can easily move out of the Prosperity paradigm and into that of Poverty without even really knowing it.

Next, when we look at any qualified retirement plan numerically, we get the following view:

Using the Qualified Plan Calculator inside the Truth Concepts Software, we'll show the whole truth around this arena. This account could be a 401(k) plan, an IRA, a SEP IRA, Simple IRA, 403(b), profit-sharing, pension plan, or anything that is under the government's domain in what are known as "Qualified Plans." Qualified Plans are all regulated by the Department of Labor and are intended to provide a tax deferral (or postponement of taxes). This calculator will tell the whole truth about the money inside this plan.

We'll look at the 401(k) first. Let's say we have an individual who is currently 35, and we're going to look out to age 64, which is 29 years. We'll use a present value (the money currently in the plan) of $100,000 and start with an earnings rate of 8 percent. It's important to understand that this is assuming a gross market rate of 8 percent every year without fluctuation; it does *not* assume an 8 percent average, as many people assume. (See page 56 for a discussion of *average* versus *actual*.) We see below that we have an account value that is going to grow to $1,006,266.

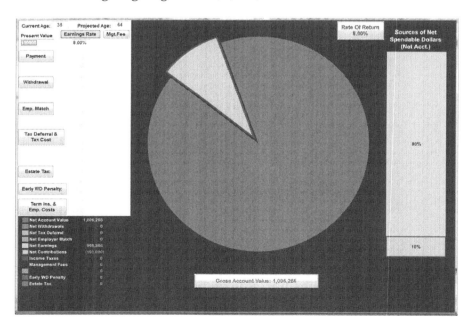

Let's also put in a level annual contribution or payment of $10,000. Notice below it didn't change our rate of return, but it did move our account value up to $2,229,724.

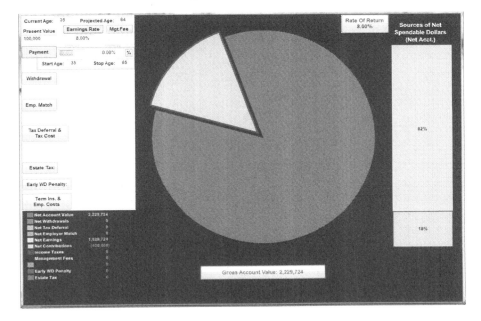

Employer Match

Now, let's think about the reasons people are tempted to put money into Qualified Retirement Plans through their employers. One of often-cited reasons for using a 401(k) is the benefit of the employer match that is often provided. We often hear people say they are getting a 50 percent match. That may be true, but you'll want to look closely at your documents, because that match often has a maximum, typically expressed as a percent of income or occasionally a flat dollar amount. In this case, let's assume the employee match is 2.5 percent of income, or $2,500, assuming this person has a gross income of $100,000. That means the actual dollar figure of the match (at 50 percent) is $1,250.

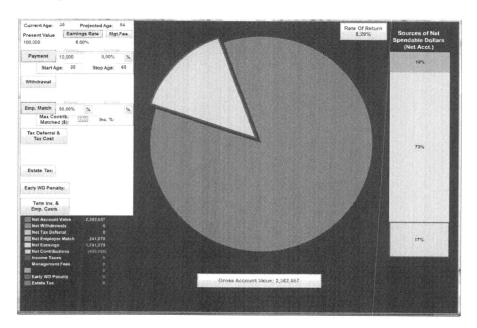

We frequently hear people say they are making money on the employer's match and that 50 percent is free money they wouldn't have had otherwise. Everyone seems to find it pretty amazing, however, that an employer match of 50 percent on up to 2.5 percent of income only increased the ROR to 8.29 percent from the 8 percent we started with. You'll notice the Gross Account Value has risen to $2,382,657.

Most people are surprised that the Rate of Return didn't go up more, especially since the match is quoted as 50 percent. While the 50 percent match increases *contributions*, it does not increase the existing *balance*. Therefore, it only slightly raises the overall rate of return.

Tax Deferral

The second reason you might be enticed to put money in your Qualified Plan is to get some tax help from the federal government. Most people look at that tax benefit as free additional dollars that go into the qualified plan. Yet in reality *it is only a tax deferral.* A tax deduction (like your mortgage interest payment) is a true deduction, whereas the tax treatment of a Qualfied Plan is to defer or postpone the taxes to an unknown time in the future and at an undisclosed rate. Confusing a tax deferral with a tax deduction is a major mistake.

So, using the federal income tax table, and acknowledging this person has Net Taxable Income (after deductions) of $80,000, we see the account value doesn't change, but the Rate of Return increases to 9.48 percent. We also see that the value of that "tax deferral" was $477,727—which represents the tax deferral plus the growth from that tax deferral at 8 percent during this timeframe. So $477,727 is the total value of having access to the government's "free" money.

It doesn't change the net account value because no additional money was deposited. This money wasn't paid in tax; it was put inside the Retirement Plan. It raises the rate of return from 8.29 percent to 9.48 percent, but it does not increase the account value. Amazing, isn't it?

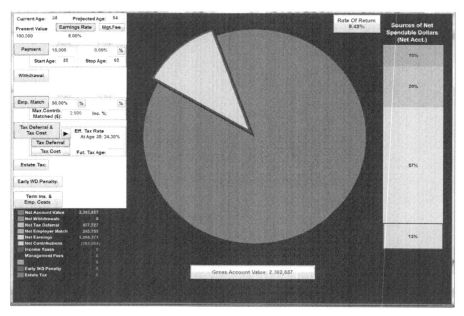

At this point in this scenario, this individual has $2,382,657 dollars in the account. We need to remember *the whole truth*—the match simply results in more dollars going *into* the account. It does NOT increase the amount in the account. Also, despite the common wisdom of those surrounding the water cooler at the office, the Tax Deferral dollars are not ours, even though they are in our account. They never were ours. They are the government's deferred tax dollars in your account that are increasing in value or losing value, right alongside your hard-earned money. So, while the match and the tax deferral do increase the Rate of Return, it has a much smaller impact than people think.

Management Fees

So now we need to start looking at the costs. When we look at a management fee, we're going to use a conservative figure of 2.5 percent. This fee covers the cost of both managing the money and administering the Qualified Retirement Plan itself. You can see below that, along the way, $439,204 was taken out of the account by management fees, bringing the account value down to $1,299,642.

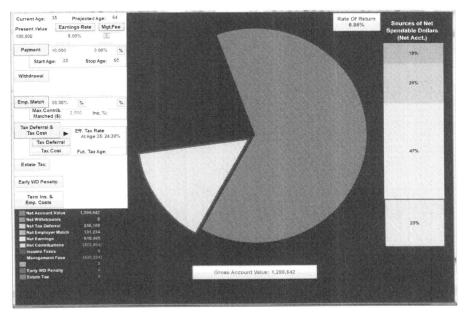

This $1,299,642 is typically the number that most people see as the value on their account statement. When people see this number, they should ask themselves, "How much of that money is mine to keep?" In reality, they only get to use that $1,299,642 if they pay the tax on it, which we'll cover shortly.

Notice that the Rate of Return is now down to 6.86 percent from the 9.48 percent we were showing earlier. This shouldn't surprise us since the fee was 2.5 percent. And remember to acknowledge that the reduction in balance is over *the full $1 million dollar account value.* Every time the fee is taken out (usually quarterly), the account balance is reduced accordingly—and thus *your earned interest and dividends are reduced.*

Again, the account was $2,382,657 before the fees and $1,299,642 afterward, for a difference of $1,083,015 lost to fees and their opportunity costs. (Opportunity costs cause the loss to be so much greater than the actual fees removed.)

Tax Cost Upon Withdrawal

Now, we'll add the cost of the tax upon withdrawal. (See graphic top of next page.) When we do, you'll see that if you liquidate the account at age 64, you would have to pay $439,954 in tax, which would leave you $859,688. (This is really the number to have in your head as the value of this account, even though the account statement is going to show the gross $1,299,642.) Looking closer at the numbers, we see that the Rate of Return is now down to 5.02 percent.

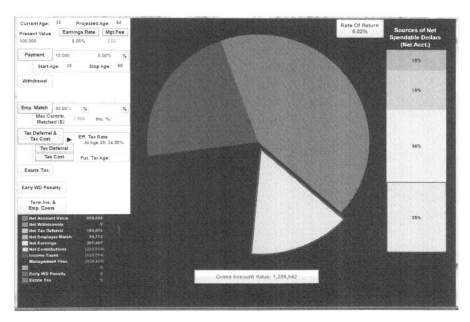

So here you are, thinking you're earning over 8 percent every year when in actuality you're earning around 5 percent. (Remember, this assumes you actually earned 8 percent each and every year—not average—that you were in the market and you had no down years.) Additionally, the lie that you have more money in your pocket because you contributed to your Qualified Plan has now been exposed.

Furthermore, you may have thought you earned money on the government's money, but in actuality, the government benefited from the growth in your qualified plan. Let's do the math on that: The tax deferral was $164,674 and you paid $439,954 in taxes. That is a $275,280 gain for the government. And you really get the whole truth of the matter when you start replacing the words "the government" in your daily discussions with the words "tax payers."

One argument we hear is that you would never take this money out in one lump sum, instead stretching it out over time. That's probably true, so let's see how this affects our rate of return. What we'll do below is change the projected age to 85. You'll notice we still show payments only though age 64. We're still going to stop contributions at age 64 but look at the scenario out to age 85. We can see this account would continue to grow and would have $3.8 million dollars in at that point. And you can see below that the Rate of Return is now showing as 5.13 percent.

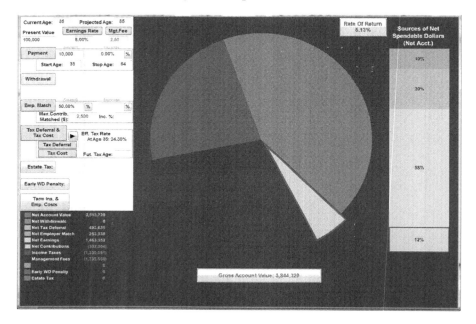

Most people are aware that taking distributions prior to reaching age 59½ will result in paying the current tax rate, plus paying a 10% "early withdrawal" penalty. Few people are aware, however, that there is an eleven-year period between 59½ and 70½ where money can be withdrawn without penalty. At age 70½, there is a 50% penalty for withdrawing less than the Required Minimum Distributions, which are determined by law. So, by law, you would have to start taking money out at age 70½ (and that may change), but we will assume annual withdrawals starting at age 65.

The calculator will automatically determine the amount this person could withdraw annually from age 65 to 85. The amount will be an annual gross income, meaning you must pay income tax on the entire amount withdrawn. The automated amount is $98,823, to be paid from the account each year, which will totally liquidate the account at age 85. The Rate of Return shows 5.46 percent. Before we calculated the annual payout, the Rate of Return was 5.13 percent. Inflation will probably cause this minor difference to be irrelevant. (The Effective Tax Rate below assumes this person continued to earn the same $80,000 net income, maybe Social Security and a pension, until age 85.)

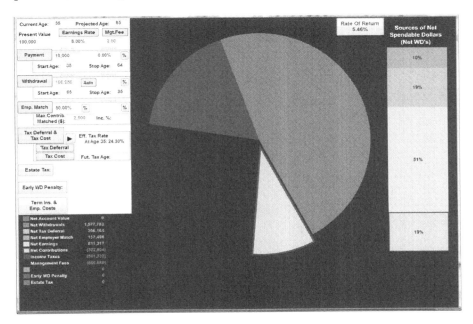

We can now see that there is not a big difference if one takes their Retirement Plan out all at once or the income gets stretched out. The impact from taxes and all other costs are still close to the same.

In this picture below, we've changed the Net Taxable Income at age 65 to $40,000 (Social Security and a pension), and you can see the Effective Tax Rate shows 21.89 percent at age 65. This boosts the rate from 5.46 to 5.65 percent—not a large improvement.

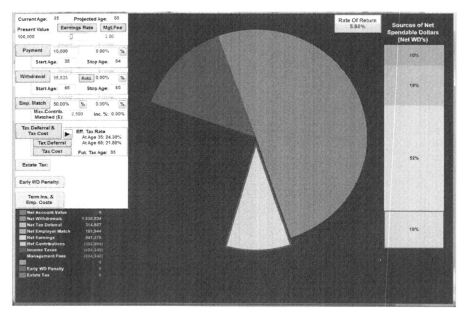

This block on the far-right column of numbers keeps track of our money—what we've actually earned in the account and what percentage it is of the net withdrawals. This breakdown shows that 19 percent of money that we spent was our own money.* Net earnings equal 52 percent on our contribution. The other 19 percent is both the tax deferral and the growth on the tax deferral by the end

---

* That was our contribution and we put in $10,000 a year, but part of that was a tax deferral so we didn't really put in the whole $10,000. The calculator only determines the Rate of Return based on our portion of the contribution into the plan (not the government-provided tax deferral). The calculation is as follows: $10,000 was the contribution, $2,430 was the tax deferral based on the 24.30 percent Effective Tax Rate from above, and the net of $7,570 is what these numbers are based on. The net of $7,570 for 30 years plus the net value of the existing $100,000 account equals the $300,984.

of the timeframe. And finally, the 10 percent is the match and the growth on that employer match. So, again, this is the breakdown of dollars we either spent or ended up with in the account.

We see a 5.65 percent Rate of Return, which tells *the whole truth* with this picture of the qualified plan and busts the retirement plan lie that the 401(k) plan is the best place to put money while one is trying to build assets. We agree that a substantial match can make this account beneficial, but for many who have a small match or none at all, tying money up until you are 59½ is not a good strategy.

The downside of a Retirement Plan (or Qualified Plan) is that they effectively eliminate your ability to use these dollars to expand on any additional opportunity that comes your way. In other words, this is all that is possible in this arena, and it doesn't look very good.

Remember, we made an assumption that you could earn 8 percent every year in the market. But what if you only earned 6 percent every year in the market with no down years?

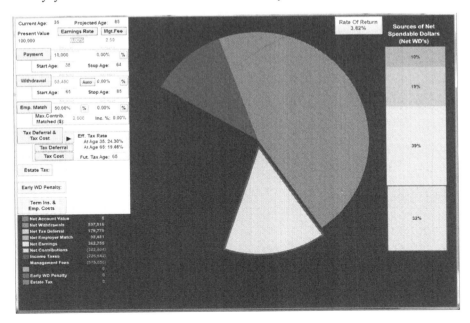

Then you would only have a 3.82 percent Rate of Return! And again, this is on money that was completely out of your control, not liquid, not available for your use, and not able to be assigned as collateral!

We use the acronym "CLUE"—Control, Liquidity, Use, and Equity—to help us remember that we would like our savings and investment strategies to be in our *control, liquid,* available for our *use,* and to act like *equity* that we could borrow against. Now, we have busted the lie that a Qualified Plan is a good place to put money.

One of our favorite books is *Life Expectancy: It's Never To Late To Change Your Game* by William Keiper. He writes, "The word 'currency' brings to mind currents: bodies of water or air moving in a specific direction, or in electricity, the flow of an electric charge through a particular medium. The word 'circulation' suggests what is really important in the pursuit of money: movement in the form of currency flowing through the entire financial system." This idea that we must stash away money for "retirement" has proven ineffective. Not only is it a bad financial choice, as we've just shown with all the Qualified Plan calculators, but it is not even good for the money! And it's not good for us in any emotional, psychological, physical, or spiritual way.

Keiper continues: "Money has no real value if it stops circulating. It may provide the holder…with a psychological benefit of security or power… but it is stuck in the system and not creating optimal value." We've preached (and practiced) the 7 Principles of Prosperity for years. As a reminder from earlier in our book: Number 5 is CONTROL, Number 6 is MOVE, and Number 7 is MULTIPLY. Typical retirement plans go against each one of those principles. You lose control, you can't move your money, and it is only doing one job (saving for retirement) when it is inside a Qualified Retirement Plan.

Keiper also writes, "Money in motion has more real value than money at rest. Money that is passing through is money that has a chance to multiply." We couldn't have said it better. And from George Orwell: "In time of universal deceit, telling the truth is a revolutionary act." We believe *Busting the Retirement Lies* not only tells the whole truth about your literally retiring (you shouldn't) but also about your finances and how saving for retirement in the typical way through Qualified Retirement Plans can actually be detrimental. (So don't!) Instead, find ways to keep your money moving through_assets, such as savings accounts inside life insurance cash value and "financial freedom" accounts in investments that are not tied up inside the government's rules about Retirement or Qualified Plans.

John C. Bogle put it best: "Give yourself all the time you can and never forget the risk of inflation." We've not calculated the impact of inflation on the Qualified Plan money in this book, but we can remind you that, while the government tells us inflation has averaged 3.23 percent from 1914–2011, they often change the "basket of goods and services" (what they use to measure inflation). This is necessary in that we no longer buy brooms, more often buying vacuums instead; however, it can also be misleading. Just know that if your money isn't going up by at least 5 percent every year, the impact of inflation is making it feel like it isn't going up at all. The only things that inflation benefits are fixed mortgage payments, fixed life insurance premiums, and people who keep on working.

"He who loves his work never labors," wrote Jim Stovall in his book *The Ultimate Gift*. "Money is nothing more than a tool. It can be a force for good, a force for evil, or simply be idle." Don't let your money or your mind be idle. Pick a project and get into it. If you don't have a project, your mind worries and worry becomes your project. Play the "Gratitude Game" by writing down everything you are grateful for, and then find one thing you can expand on and go do that. Then pick the next thing and go do that.

Steve Chandler, in his book *Wealth Warrior: The Personal Prosperity Revolution*, writes that, in order to get out of a mental rut, you must start some action. "The action itself is what starts the fire and creates the passion in you, along with the desire to do great work. Follow your effort and you'll find your passion."

Average Versus Actual

It's important to cover one last point before we close this chapter—the fallacy of "Average Rates of Return." These are often touted by financial experts, and yet simple math can show us that *average* does not equal *actual*.

Pretend that you invested $100,000 into a mutual fund that had promised an average rate of return of 25 percent if you left the money alone for two years. In the first year, it earned 100 percent, after which, the investment would look like this:

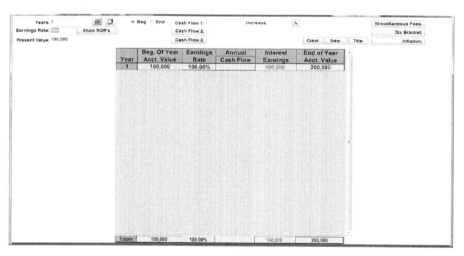

In the second year, the fund earned -50 percent (that is negative 50 percent), and so now your investment looks like this:

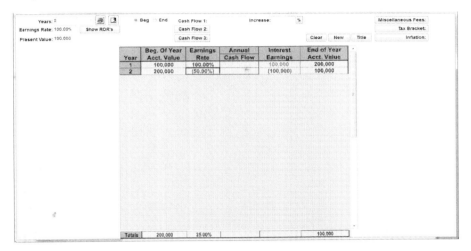

While your funds average was 25 percent (that is mathematically correct: 100 percent plus negative 50 percent divided by 2 years equals 25 percent), its actual yield was 0 percent because you ended up with only the $100,000 you started with.

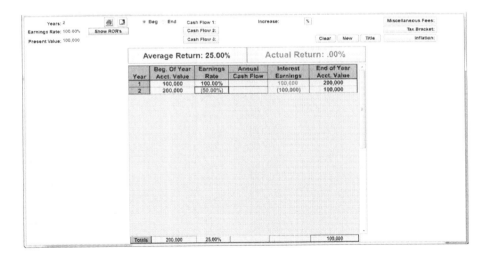

This simple but clear example shows how "average" does not equal "actual"—so you will always want to know what the *actual* return on your money is.

>>>>>> CHAPTER 6

THINK ABOUT LIVING TO 100+

"Retirement kills more people than hard work ever did."

—*Malcolm Forbes*

Did you know, there are more than half a million centenarians in the world today? And that number is only expected to increase in coming years.

The United Kingdom's Office of National Statistics has forecasted that 35% of those "born in 2012 will live to become centenarians," according to a report in *The Guardian* (March 6, 2012). And Fox News reported on a 2009 article in the famed medical research journal, *The Lancet*, citing research that "life expectancy is increasing steadily in most countries, even beyond the limits of what scientists first thought possible." (http://www.foxnews.com/story/0,2933,558964,00.html#ixzz241bhd8yg)

In fact, according to Dr. Henry Lodge, in his book *Younger Next Year*, "It turns out that 70% of American aging is not real aging. It's just decay. It's rot from the stuff that we do. All the lifestyle diseases… diabetes, obesity, heart disease, alzheimers, cancers etc.… those are all decay. Nature doesn't have that in store for any of us. We go and buy it off the rack."

According to Steve Franklin, an educator, author, and entrepreneur, "Research suggests that centenarians have been doubling in number every decade since the 1950s and that by 2050, there will be close to 1,000,000 American centenarians, making it the fastest growing age segment in our population." Dr. Franklin, who says he wants to live to at least 120, has launched The Centenarian Project, to capture what he calls "authentic wisdom from America's centenarians." The site makes for fascinating reading and viewing—www.100Wisdom.com.

When we start thinking about our lives in terms of 100+ years, many things take on a whole new meaning. For example, if you have a long-term project, knowing that you may have many more years on earth helps you tackle it in a patient way. Not feeling like you have to get it done this weekend enables you to enjoy the process more, smell the roses (and feel the thorns) along the way, and do a better job by taking the time to do it right. In our "fast-food society," we expect things overnight when a 20- or 30-year perspective might help us to not only enjoy the journey, but also end up feeling better about the results along the way.

One of the ways you can institute this in your life is to adopt a new time-management system. For example, Dan Sullivan, founder of The Strategic Coach® Inc., created a time-management system called The Entrepreneurial Time System®. This system helps entrepreneurs gain an ever-increasing amount of personal freedom, while generating the greatest possible results for their businesses. At its core, it completely alters an individual's relationship to time—dividing life into three distinct types of days, which are referred to as Free, Focus, and Buffer Days®.

But you don't have to be an entrepreneur to take advantage of the concept. The basic idea is to split your time into three distinct "black and white" days instead of having all your days be "grey."

A typical retiree treats every day the same: doing a few chores, having a fun outing, killing some time reading, and then getting up the next day and doing it all over again. This might work well for a few months, but after a while it can get boring.

Instead, consider putting all your "chore" work into one day. We'll call this the *Focus Day*. You are expected to get results—so get up, go to "work," and get it done.

Then, strategize one full day for fun. This will be your *Free Day*. Literally, from the time you wake up until the time you go to bed, only do things that you totally love and get you energized.

Then, plan a *Buffer Day* in the middle, before each of your Focus or Free Days, where you do all the things to prepare for a great Focus Day (like go to the store, get your hair cut, etc.) and all the things to prepare for a great Free Day (like find the map for a hike, get all the food ready, etc).

The definitions of each day will differ for one person to another. For example, mowing the lawn for one person may be considered a fun activity, while to another it's a chore. So only you can say what you want to plan on your Free Days, Focus Days, and Buffer Days. Additionally, if there is a "significant other" in your house (spouse or otherwise) you'll want to plan days so that you spend some together, some apart, and most importantly, all of them as coordinated as possible.

Retirement Profile: Viktor Frankl (1905–1997) Choose Your Attitude!

Life today is tough, no question. So many of us deal with economic and financial stress and constraints, families that are broken apart or scattered, careers that may not be our first choice, governments that may be inefficient or corrupt.... So, when we feel despondent, angry, even bitter, hopeless, it's justified, right?

Wrong!

Take the example of Viktor Frankl—if ever there was a man who had the right to feel all these feelings and carry them through life, that man was Dr. Frankl. A brilliant, inquiring mind, with a brilliant career in psychoanalysis before him, Frankl's world came crashing down with the advent of Nazism in his native Austria. He endured three years at the infamous Auschwitz concentration camp, where his pregnant wife was sent to the gas chambers. Frankl's mother, father, and brother suffered the same fate. (Only his sister survived, who had fortunately emigrated to Australia several years before World War II.)

And Frankl survived—without bitterness and rancor. After being liberated from the camps, he chose to remain in Austria. He also chose *not* to remain a prisoner of his horrific past, but instead to wring meaning and learning from it and share that with the wider world. He dictated his most famous book, *Man's Search for Meaning*, in a period of less than two weeks. In this book, he observed, "Everything can be taken from a man, but one thing: the last of the human freedoms—to choose one's attitude in any given set of circumstances, to choose one's own way."

Looking back on his experiences in the camp, he said, "It did not really matter what we expected from life, but rather what life expected from us." And, looking forward, he noted, "We can discover meaning in life in three different ways: (1) by creating a work or doing a deed; (2) by experiencing something or encountering someone; and (3) by the attitude we take toward unavoidable suffering."

Even before his transformative experiences in the concentration camps, Frankl had "evolved the theory . . . that the search for value and meaning in the circumstance of one's life was the key to psychological well-being." (*The New York Times*, September 4, 1997)

And there's ample proof, in that he lived to the age of 95, actively teaching, debating, thinking and contributing to society.

Retirement Profile: R. Nelson Nash (1931–)
"Life Is Too Much Fun to Miss Out!"

Octogenarian R. Nelson Nash is a man who doesn't believe in retirement. "There is no way to convince me to retire! This life is too much fun to miss out!" he exclaimed in a recent interview with the *Lara-Murphy Report*. ("Austrian Economics + Whole Life = Infinite Banking Concept," December 2011, pp. 19-23.)

The originator of the Infinite Banking Concept, which promotes the use of whole life insurance as a way to finance one's major expenses, Mr. Nash is an active speaker, writer, and contributor to various publications.

In his view, the very idea of retirement is an anomaly. First, he says, "Mankind needs purpose in life." And, just as important, retirement ages as legislated by government are arbitrary. Germany's Chancellor Bismarck has the dubious distinction of starting the convention of retirement and social security—which he set for 70 years of age, when the average life expectancy was well below that. Similarly, Nash says, when Social Security was introduced in the United States in 1937, with the age of retirement being deemed 65, the average life expectancy was 61 years. Today, for Americans, life expectancy is closer to 79–80 years. Thus, Nash believes, there is no way Social Security can ever really work in the long term and give "retired" people an adequate living income.

Nash, a longtime friend and colleague of the author, started his career as a forester for private companies in the early 1950s, after graduating with a Bachelor of Science Degree in Forestry from the University of Georgia. He also served as a life insurance agent with Equitable of New York for 23 years and The Guardian Life for 12 years. His concept of Infinite Banking is described in his classic book, *Becoming Your Own Banker*, and is the basis for about 50 seminars a year around the United States. To find out more about Nash's strategy, go to the website www.InfiniteBanking.org.

(Incidentally, the Prosperity Economic Movement supports the use of whole life insurance as a place to store cash and borrow against when needed.)

CHAPTER 7

LIVE AND SHARE WITH PASSION

"When you retire, think and act as if you were still working; when you're still working, think and act a bit as if you were already retired."

—*Unknown*

We feel strongly that too many families let long periods of time go by where life is merely happening to them. This is easy to do with our busy schedules, yet it can lead to a sense of "Where does the time go?" and "Why don't I ever get to do what I want, or do something fun?"

So our suggestion is to make a list of fun things you'd like to do—a "bucket list" of sorts—but don't wait until "retirement" to start doing some of those things. (If you'd like some ideas, and a good laugh in the bargain, you may want to watch the 2007 Rob Reiner movie, *The Bucket List*, starring Morgan Freeman and Jack Nicholson.)

On this list, we encourage you to write in some challenges. Your brain and your muscles live in a "use it or lose it environment," so pick a new thing to learn every year from the list. It works even better if your spouse would enjoy learning the same thing, too. To assist with this, MarriageBuilders.com has a "Recreational Enjoyment Inventory" questionnaire. Go to the site and search "REI."

Human beings were built to push our limits a bit, so consider pushing yourself at least once each week—mentally, by doing something you aren't comfortable with; physically, by doubling your workout for a day; emotionally, by reaching out to someone who you wouldn't have otherwise; and/or spiritually, by doubling your prayer or meditation time.

Consider the concept of **both**—rather than either/or! How often do we humans strategize for "A" *or* "B" instead of "A" *and* "B"? Consider adopting the idea of trying to get BOTH. Strategize the various things you want to do or items you'd like to have and see if you can pull them BOTH off. This will keep you thinking, and keep you excited and upbeat. When you are excited, others feel this. Excitement is contagious—and it won't hurt others to catch it!

Focus on *adding* to your health, rather than what you can't do. Add walking, water, or weights, etc., rather than trying to "lose weight" or "stop drinking coffee." The positive focus is much better and you'll get better results. Here's the Prosperity Economics Movement founder's list of positive changes she's working on:

More	Less
Books	Magazines
Movies	TV
Water	Soda
Tea	Coffee
Veggies	Chips
Love	Resentment
Walking	Sitting
Saving	Spending
Recreation	Shopping
Gratitude	Complaining
Humility	Ego
Flow	Resistance

Top 10 Tips for Staying Young Physically
by Nancy Riedmann McVeigh, personal trainer

1. Get a good night's sleep.
2. Stretch—it keeps the body limber and decreases your chance of injury.
3. Drink lots of water.
4. Eat a nutritious breakfast that includes protein and carbohydrates.
5. Eat high-fiber foods and limit foods high in saturated fat and sugar.
6. Have good posture—don't slouch.
7. Set goals to keep learning and growing.
8. Be physically active each day, doing something you enjoy.
9. Smile and be happy— it can be contagious.
10. Learn how to manage stress in healthy ways.

> "The biggest motivation I have to keep competing is that I feel I am improving."
>
> — *Japanese equestrian Hiroshi Hoketsu, who at age 71 was the oldest Olympian in London. He competed first in the Tokyo Games in 1964, then 44 years later in Beijing, and most recently in London in 2012, where he placed 17th in the individual dressage event.*

Retirement Profile: Steven R. Covey (1932–2012) "Sharpen That Saw!"

Chances are, you've probably heard of Steven Covey and his long-time best-selling book, *7 Habits of Highly Effective People*. A leader in the field of self-help publishing and coaching, Dr. Covey's work has been transformative for millions—and informed his long and productive career.

Until his unexpected passing (as the result of a bicycle accident) in July 2012, the 79-year-old Covey exemplified the maxims of self-reliance and focus that he urged on readers. His advice and ideas, which led to the building of his multi-million-dollar publishing empire, focused almost exclusively on character, things each of us can control and influence within ourselves. Not much that Covey wrote about is new or "rocket science"; most of it is common sense. But it's common sense that we seem to have forgotten or think is no longer relevant.

In short, Covey promoted the following seven "habits":

1. Be proactive.
2. Begin with the end in mind.
3. Put first things first.
4. Think win/win.
5. Seek first to understand, then to be understood.
6. Synergize.
7. Sharpen the saw

This last of the seven habits is an injunction to seek constantly to improve oneself—mentally, physically, technically—which is especially important for people as they advance in age, since staying active and striving for improvement has a demonstrated connection to health and longevity.

Though aimed primarily at those wanting to progress in the realm of business, these principles can be applied to virtually every aspect of our lives—and at any stage in our lives. Covey certainly practiced what he preached, making an active contribution throughout his life—and longer, as his wisdom lives on in his writings.

Retirement Profile: Tom Peters (1942–)
Still Pursuing "Excellence"!

If Steven Covey was the guru of personal development, then Tom Peters—whose seminal work, *In Search of Excellence*, preceded Covey's by nearly a decade—is the guru of professional development.

At nearly 70 years old, Peters has been contemplating his extraordinarily productive and busy life as a management consultant and motivational expert, following a health challenge (necessitating a pacemaker) a few years ago. Peters took the opportunity to reflect on the concept of "retirement" and "slowing down." According to an in-depth article in *U.S. News & World Report* (September 1, 2010), Peters "has been asking himself the same questions as millions of others who are in or nearing the traditional age of retirement."

Well known for working long, punishing hours and thriving on a schedule that would make many others quail, Peters is now seizing the opportunity to reevaluate priorities. For those in the working world, his book *Talent: Develop It, Sell It, Be It*, warns, "The microchip will colonize all rote activities. And we will have to scramble to reinvent ourselves—as we did when we came off the farm and went into the factory, and then as we were ejected from the factory and delivered to the white-collar towers.... The reinvented you and the reinvented me will have no choice but to scramble and add value in some meaningful way."

But, when it comes to the typical retirement years, Peters has a different take on staying useful and productive—when speaking for himself, at least. "Statistically and emotionally, I believe that the way I can be of help to society is by doing what I know and what I've been good at," the *U.S. News* article quotes Peters as saying.

More of his advice relates to jumping into something brand new right away. To quote the article: "when you make an enormous transition [in working life], you really have to be careful not to find another way to work 18 hours a day, six days a week doing something else.... Immediately finding a way to fill your time is really, really bad news."

LOOKING AHEAD

As we bring this book to a close, we want to share with you one more inspirational story about someone who didn't know the meaning of retirement.

You may have heard of American-born Sir John Marks Templeton (1912–2008), founder and leader of one of the most successful private financial services companies in the world. One thing that kept him active and interested in life, his entire life, was his tendency to go against the flow. For example: "In September 1939, when the war-spooked world was selling, he borrowed $10,000 to buy 100 shares in everything that was trading for less than a dollar a share on the New York Stock Exchange. All but four eventually turned profits. In early 2000, conversely, he sold all his dotcom and Nasdaq tech stocks just before the market crashed. His iron principle of investing was 'to buy when others are despondently selling and to sell when others are greedily buying.' At the point of 'maximum pessimism' he would enter, and clean up." (*The Economist*, July 27, 2008.)

And yet Sir Templeton's enthusiasm for life wasn't confined

to the world of finance (nor to his younger years). In 1973, at age 61, he started the annual Templeton Prize for Progress in Religion, awarded for individual achievement in "life's spiritual dimension," which he felt had too long been disregarded. Then in 1987, at the age of 75, he set up the Templeton Foundation to promote thoughtful inquiry into the subject of God and religious and spiritual life. But, according to his obituary in *The Daily Telegraph*, "this was only a drop in the ocean of Templeton's philanthropy. He endowed university courses in spirituality and science, funded medical schools to run classes on healing and spirituality, and rewarded universities and individuals that upheld 'traditional educational values,' schools that promoted 'character development,' and colleges that taught market economics."

One example of his philanthropic impact is cited as well in *The Economist* article: "You could give away too much land and too much money, said Sir John, but never enough love, and the real return was immediate: more love. The Institute for Research on Unlimited Love, founded with his money, was set up to study this dynamic of the spiritual marketplace." Over a decade after the institute's start, it is going strong and making a difference.

Even into his 90s, Sir Templeton never retired. Every day, he took "power walks" against the ocean current by his Bermuda home, kept up with the markets and their impact on the philanthropic foundation he had established, and pondered questions about man's spiritual nature.

Now, as you can see, Templeton certainly did not fit the "average retiree" profile:

A. He was several decades past the age when the typical person would have stopped working productively; and

B. He was immensely wealthy to boot.

So, he really didn't need to work at all. Ever. But he chose to. What a perfect example of busting the retirement lie!

We urge you to reconsider retirement—and even refuse to go along with the accepted traditions and expectations of a decline in activity, productivity, and purpose. Each of you, each of us, still has much to give—and much to learn. And, as we've seen with increasing life expectancies worldwide, we now have more time in which to learn life's glorious lessons.

Thus, our recommendation to you, broken down by age range:

- For those of you early in your careers (ages 20–35), keep seeking work you love so you can do that work for as long as possible.
- For those of you in the middle (ages 35–55), if you don't love your work, find other work—because you will want to be doing that work for many more years. If you do happen to enjoy your work, congratulations! Keep at it while taking long weekends, vacations, and even sabbaticals along the way, just keep working.
- For those of you ages 55–70, take some vacations, take long weekends, and be well-rested—so you can envision working for a longer period in your life than you had originally thought. (As we learned at the end of Chapter 6 that Tom Peters is doing with his life.)
- For those of you already retired and loving it, keep doing what you're doing!
- And last, for those of you retired and not loving it, find a way to provide value—this is what will get you excited again! It may take a few starts and stops until you find "your thing," but it will be well worth it.

RESOURCE GUIDE

BOOKS

Don't Retire, REWIRE!
Jeri Sedlar and Rick Miners, ALPHA, second edition, 2007

LIFE Expectancy: It's Never Too Late to Change Your Game
William Keiper, FirstGlobal Partners LLC, 2012

The Ultimate Gift
Jim Stovall, David C. Cook (Publisher), 2007

Wealth Warrior: The Personal Prosperity Revolution
Steve Chandler, Maurice Bassett (Publisher), 2012

God Wants You to be Rich
Paul Zane Pilzer, Simon and Schuster, 1995

Growing Old Is Not for Sissies (1 & 2)
Etta Clark, Pomegranate Publishers, 1986

Younger Next Year: Live Strong, Fit, and Sexy—Until You're 80 and Beyond
Dr. Henry Lodge and Chris Crowley, Workman Publishing, 2007

Busting the Financial Planning Lies: Learn to Use Prosperity Economics to Build Sustainable Wealth, Prosperity Economics Movement, 2012

PERSONAL/PROFESSIONAL DEVELOPMENT WEBSITES

www.Kolbe.com

www.InstinctiveLife.com

www.StrategicCoach.com

www.StrengthsFinder.com

www.TruthConcepts.com

NETWORKING & VOLUNTEERING WEBSITES

www.NetworkForGood.org
Helps people connect with a cause

www.VolunteerMatch.org
Matches you to volunteer opportunities

www.PartnersInCare.org
Volunteer seniors use their time and talents to help others and, in exchange, receive help when they need it (only available in Maryland)

www.VocationVacations.com
Try a dream vocation on vacation!

www.Freelance.com
Freelance work opportunities

www.RetiredBrains.com
www.RetiredJobs.com
www.SeniorJobBank.com
www.Seniors4Hire.com
The sites above help older workers find jobs

www.SeniorNet.org
Computer technology and Internet training

www.Eons.com
Everything for people over 50

www.SeniorsHelpingSeniors.com
See profile on page 9

ADDITIONAL ONLINE INFORMATION

http://rss.csmonitor.com/~r/feeds/csm/~3/ourlkr2To2c/Why-we-work-and-keep-working

http://www.csmonitor.com/USA/Society/2012/0902/The-silver-collar-economy

http://www.csmonitor.com/World/Asia-Pacific/2012/0902/In-Japan-better-with-age

FILMS

The Ultimate Gift (based on the book by Jim Stovall)
Directed by Michael O. Sajbel, 2006

The Best Exotic Marigold Hotel
Directed by John Madden, 2011

Ghost Town
Directed by David Koepp, 2008

The Prosperity Economics Movement is a non-profit organization comprising financial experts who practice Prosperity Economics and individuals who would like to learn how to apply the principles of Prosperity Economics to improve their lives. This book is part of a growing body of information that will support the organization and its members.

To learn more or buy your own copy of this book, go to:
www.MountainTopsEducation.com

Made in the USA
Charleston, SC
17 January 2013